Fabulous Flower Quilts
by Bea Yurkerwich

Chitra Publications

Montrose, Pennsylvania
Your Best Value in Quilting
www.QuiltTownUSA.com

—— In loving memory of my parents, Helen and John Stone ——

Introduction

Bringing a beautiful flower quilt into your home is like having a year-round garden. Like gardening, quiltmaking is both meditative and fulfilling. Both activities can bring great serenity into the lives of those who enjoy doing them. Regardless of your skill level as a quiltmaker, you'll be able to piece the floral designs presented in this book.

In 1985, I bought a quilted pillow kit. By the time I finished it, the "quilting bug" had bitten me. I knew I wanted to be a quiltmaker! I loved selecting the fabrics with so many wonderful colors and prints—and what a vast array from which to choose! After making several traditional quilts, I started to design and draft my own quilt patterns, an aspect of quiltmaking that I have come to enjoy more than any other.

Gentle Geometrics

I call my style of designing "Gentle Geometrics" because the sewing lines have straight stitching although the flowers, leaves, and other shapes appear to be curved, and from a distance they have a soft, natural look. I use graph paper with 1/4" grids to create design elements that usually are squares, triangles, and rectangles. I almost always use a set of small hinged mirrors during the design process. After sketching and coloring the blocks, I place mirrors at the top and left of the block to instantly see what the blocks will look like when set together. At the center where four blocks meet, a secondary design often comes into play, resulting in a wonderful optical-illusion.

In addition to making the full-size quilts from this book, I encourage you to use a block from any of the designs to make a pillowtop or a small wallhanging. Whether you are just learning to quilt or are an experienced quilter, I think you'll find these designs will bring inspiration and enjoyment to your quiltmaking endeavors for years to come. Making a beautiful floral quilt will be a joy forever.

Happy quilting!

Dedication

To my husband, Robert Peter Yurkerwich, for his loving encouragement and help in every way throughout our years together. He is my official "Stitch-Outie" (expert seam ripper) and has taken out nearly as many stitches as I have sewn! He also winds bobbins for me, a dozen colors at a time, and taught me computer skills so this book could be written! (In addition, he also picks up hundreds of small pieces of fabric and thread that seem to migrate mysteriously to all parts of the house, not just the sewing area!) Thank you for everything, Bob.

Contents

Tulip Whirl 4

Golden Sunflowers 7

Dancing Flowers
and Pinwheels 11

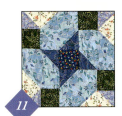

Star Magnolia 14

Friendship Star Flower 18

Pinwheel Garden 21

Iris Garden 24

Circle of Tulips 29

Acknowledgements

A heartfelt thank you to all our family and friends for their encouragement and enthusiasm for my designs, especially my sisters, Louise Woodward and Lea Avertin, and our good friend, Glenna Ketchum, for her computer expertise. Thanks to my husband, Bob, for helping me find entire paragraphs that disappeared into cyberspace!

A special thank you to the talented quiltmakers Daryl Dowding, Jennifer Kay, Anne Pollard, and Robby Wargny for making the beautiful quilts in this book by following my colored drawings and directions. To Kathy Stewart and Diane Luken (Thimbles & Thread Quilt Shop) who did the beautiful machine quilting and binding on Golden Sunflowers. My heart is filled with joy and gratitude to each and every one of you.

"WHEREVER YOUR LIVES MAY BE CAST, MAKE YOU THE WORLD A BIT BETTER AND MORE BEAUTIFUL, BECAUSE YOU LIVED IN IT." —*Edward William Bok • Lake Wales, Florida*

Tulip Whirl

The whirlwind of brightly colored tulips and Pinwheels stirs the imagination.
A secondary design of lighter Pinwheels is formed when four blocks are set together.

TULIP WHIRL

Quilt Size: 56" square • Block Size: 16" square

Materials

- 2 yards yellow
- 3/4 yard medium green
- 1/4 yard dark green
- 1 yard red
- 1 3/4 yards dark blue floral
- 1/4 yard medium blue
- 3/8 yard light blue
- 1 yard white
- 3 1/2 yards backing fabric
- 60" square of batting

Cutting

Dimensions include a 1/4" seam allowance. Cut the lengthwise dark blue floral strips before cutting other pieces from the same fabric.

From the yellow:
- Cut 6: 2 1/2" x 40" strips, for the binding
- Cut 18: 4 7/8" squares, then cut them in half diagonally to yield 36 triangles
- Cut 108: 2 1/2" squares
- Cut 18: 2 7/8" squares
- Cut 36: 2 1/2" x 4 1/2" rectangles

From the medium green:
- Cut 36: 2 1/2" x 6 1/2" rectangles
- Cut 36: 2 1/2" squares

From the dark green:
- Cut 36: 2 1/2" squares

From the red:
- Cut 36: 2 1/2" x 4 1/2" rectangles
- Cut 18: 2 7/8" squares

From the dark blue floral:
- Cut 4: 4 1/2" x 58" lengthwise strips
- Cut 36: 2 1/2" x 4 1/2" rectangles

From the medium blue:
- Cut 18: 2 7/8" squares, then cut them in half diagonally to yield 36 triangles

From the light blue:
- Cut 9: 5 1/4" squares, then cut them in quarters diagonally to yield 36 triangles

From the white:
- Cut 36: 2 1/2" x 4 1/2" rectangles
- Cut 36: 2 1/2" squares
- Cut 18: 2 7/8" squares, then cut them in half diagonally to yield 36 triangles

Directions

1. Sew a medium blue triangle to a white triangle to make a pieced triangle.

2. Sew the pieced triangle to a light blue triangle. Sew the unit to a yellow triangle to make a corner unit. Make 36.

3. Draw a diagonal line from corner to corner on the wrong side of the 2 1/2" white squares, 2 1/2" medium green squares, 2 1/2" dark green squares, 2 7/8" yellow squares, and thirty-six 2 1/2" yellow squares.

4. Place a marked 2 1/2" yellow square on a 2 1/2" x 4 1/2" red rectangle. Sew on the drawn line. Press the square toward the corner, aligning the edges. Trim the seam allowance to 1/4". Make 36.

5. Place a marked 2 7/8" yellow square on a 2 7/8" red square, right sides together. Sew 1/4" away from

TULIP WHIRL

the drawn line on both sides. Make 18.

6. Cut the squares on the drawn lines to yield 36 pieced squares.

7. Sew a pieced square to a 2 1/2" yellow square. Sew the unit to a pieced rectangle to make a Bud unit. Make 36.

8. Place a 2 1/2" x 4 1/2" yellow rectangle on a 2 1/2" x 6 1/2" medium green rectangle, aligning the edges, as shown. Sew from corner to corner. Trim 1/4" beyond the stitching. Press the seam allowance toward the green.

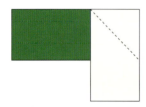

9. Place a marked 2 1/2" white square on the opposite end of the medium green rectangle. Sew on the drawn line. Press the square toward the corner and trim the seam allowance to 1/4". Make 36.

10. Place a 2 1/2" x 4 1/2" white rectangle on a 2 1/2" x 4 1/2" dark blue floral rectangle, aligning the edges.

Sew from corner to corner and trim, as before. Press the seam allowance toward the white. Trim.

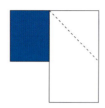

11. Place a marked medium green square on the dark blue floral end of the pieced rectangle, and a marked dark green square on the white end. Sew the squares from corner to corner. Press the squares toward the corners and trim the seam allowances to 1/4". Make 36.

12. Sew a 2 1/2" yellow square to the dark green end of each pieced strip.

13. Lay out 2 pieced strips, a bud unit, and a corner unit. Join them to make a quarter block. Make 36.

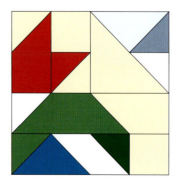

Assembly

1. Lay out 4 quarter blocks and join them as shown to make a block.

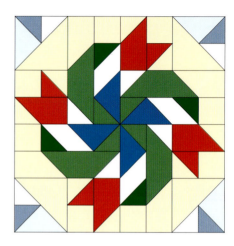

2. Lay out the blocks in 3 rows of 3. Sew the blocks into rows and join the rows.

3. Center and stitch the 4 1/2" x 58" dark blue floral strips to the sides of the quilt. Start, stop, and backstitch at the 1/4" seamlines.

4. Miter the corners as described in the *General Directions*.

5. Finish the quilt as described in the *General Directions*, using the 2 1/2" x 40" yellow strips for the binding.

Golden Sunflowers

*The radiant blooms of "**Golden Sunflowers**" are like an inviting smile. This cheerful wallhanging always reminds me of summer's warm sunny days.*

Golden Sunflowers

Quilt Size: 54" square • Block Size: 20" square

Materials

- 1/2 yard yellow
- 1/2 yard medium gold
- 1/4 yard dark gold
- 1/4 yard brown
- 1/3 yard medium green
- 1/3 yard dark green
- 1 1/4 yards light aqua
- 1 3/4 yards dark aqua
- 1/8 yard dark blue
- 1 3/4 yards white
- 3 1/2 yards backing fabric
- 58" square of batting

Cutting

Patterns (page 10 and 17) are full size and include a 1/4" seam allowance as do all dimensions given.

From the yellow:
- Cut 16: A
- Cut 16: AR

From the medium gold:
- Cut 16: B
- Cut 16: BR

From the dark gold:
- Cut 8: 3 1/4" squares, then cut them in quarters diagonally to yield 32 triangles

From the brown:
- Cut 4: C

From the medium green:
- Cut 4: 2 1/2" x 10 1/2" strips
- Cut 4: 2 1/2" x 8 1/2" strips

From the dark green:
- Cut 4: 2 1/2" x 8 1/2" strips
- Cut 4: 2 1/2" x 4 1/2" strips

From the light aqua:
- Cut 16: 2 1/2" x 4 1/2" strips
- Cut 16: 4 1/2" squares

- Cut 12: 2 1/2" x 20 1/2" strips

From the dark aqua:
- Cut 4: 2 1/2" x 58" lengthwise strips, for the binding
- Cut 2: 4 1/2" x 56" lengthwise strips
- Cut 2: 4 1/2" x 48" lengthwise strips
- Cut 16: 2 1/2" squares

From the dark blue:
- Cut 9: 2 1/2" squares, for the cornerstones

From the white:
- Cut 32: 2 7/8" squares, then cut them in half diagonally to yield 64 large triangles
- Cut 8: 3 1/4" squares, then cut them in quarters diagonally to yield 32 small triangles
- Cut 8: 2 1/2" x 12 1/2" strips
- Cut 16: 2 1/2" x 10 1/2" strips
- Cut 16: 2 1/2" x 8 1/2" strips
- Cut 8: 2 1/2" x 4 1/2" strips
- Cut 12: 2 1/2" squares

Directions

1. Lay out a medium gold B, 2 large white triangles, a yellow A, a small white triangle, and a dark gold triangle. Sew them into sections as shown. Join the sections to make a pieced triangle. Make 16.

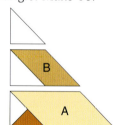

2. Lay out a medium gold BR, 2 large white triangles, a yellow AR, a small white triangle, and a dark gold triangle. Sew them into sections. Join the sections to make a reverse pieced triangle. Make 16.

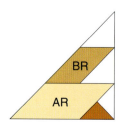

3. Sew a pieced triangle and a reverse pieced triangle together to make a quarter unit. Make 16.

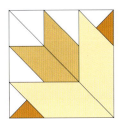

4. Sew 4 quarter units together to make a Sunflower. Make 4.

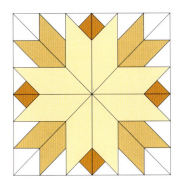

5. Draw a diagonal line from corner to corner on the wrong side of each 2 1/2" white square.

6. Place a marked square on each end of a 2 1/2" x 8 1/2" dark green strip, as shown. Sew on the drawn lines. Press the squares toward the corners and trim the seam allowances to 1/4". Make 4.

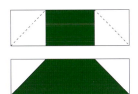

7. Place a marked square on a 2 1/2" x 10 1/2" medium green strip, as shown. Sew on the drawn line. Press and trim, as before. Make 4.

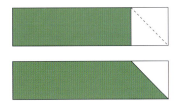

8. Place a medium green unit on a dark green unit, aligning the bottom right corners, as shown. Sew from corner to corner. Open the unit and press the seam toward the medium green. Trim the seam allowance to 1/4" to complete a top leaf unit. Make 4. Set them aside.

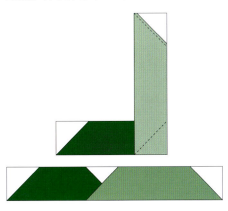

9. Place a 2 1/2" x 4 1/2" dark green strip on a 2 1/2" x 4 1/2" white strip, as shown. Sew from corner to corner. Open the unit and press the seam toward the dark green. Trim, as before. Make 4.

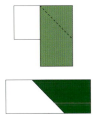

10. Place a 2 1/2" x 4 1/2" white strip on a 2 1/2" x 8 1/2" medium green strip, as shown. Sew from corner to corner. Open the unit and press the seam toward the medium green. Trim. Make 4.

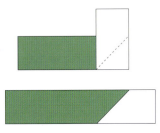

11. Join 2 units to make a bottom leaf unit, as shown. Make 4.

12. Sew a bottom leaf unit to a top leaf unit. Make 4.

13. Sew 2 1/2" x 12 1/2" white strips to the left and right side of each Sunflower. Sew a leaf section to the bottom.

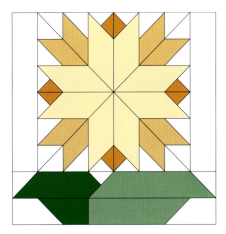

14. Appliqué a brown circle (C) over the center of each block.

15. Place a 2 1/2" x 4 1/2" light aqua strip on a 2 1/2" x 8 1/2" white strip. Sew from corner to corner. Press the seam toward the aqua. Trim the seam allowance to 1/4".

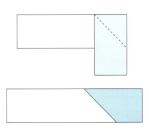

16. Place a 2 1/2" x 8 1/2" white strip on the other end of the aqua strip.

Golden Sunflowers

Sew from corner to corner. Press the seam toward the aqua to complete a pieced strip. Trim the seam allowance to 1/4". Make 8.

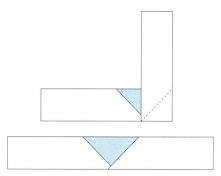

17. Make 8 pieced strips in the same manner, using the 2 1/2" x 10 1/2" white strips and the remaining 2 1/2" x 4 1/2" light aqua strips.

18. Sew short pieced strips to the left and right sides of a block. Sew long pieced strips to the top and bottom. Make 4.

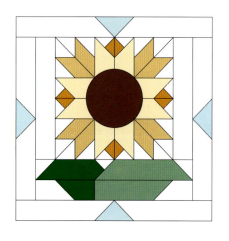

19. Draw a diagonal line from corner to corner on the wrong side of each 4 1/2" light aqua square and each 2 1/2" dark aqua square.

20. Place a marked light aqua square on each corner of a block. Sew on the drawn lines. Press the squares toward the corners, aligning the edges. Trim the seam allowances to 1/4".

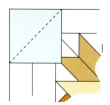

21. Place a marked dark aqua square on each corner of a block. Sew on the drawn lines. Press and trim to complete a block. Make 4.

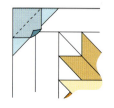 

Assembly

1. Lay out the blocks, 2 1/2" x 20 1/2" light aqua strips, and 2 1/2" dark blue cornerstones.

2. Sew the blocks and vertical strips into 2 rows. Sew the cornerstones and horizontal strips into 3 pieced strips. Join the rows and strips.

3. Measure the length of the quilt. Trim the 4 1/2" x 48" dark aqua strips to that measurement. Sew them to the sides of the quilt.

4. Measure the width of the quilt, including the borders. Trim the 4 1/2" x 56" dark aqua strips to that measurement. Sew them to the top and bottom of the quilt.

5. Finish the quilt as described in the *General Directions*, using the 2 1/2" x 58" dark aqua strips for the binding.

Full-Size Patterns for Golden Sunflowers

(Patterns continued on page 17)

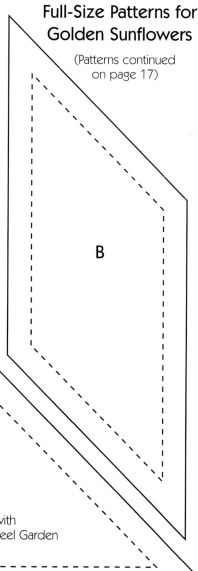

Use pattern piece A with Golden Sunflowers and Pinwheel Garden

Dancing Flowers and Pinwheels

*Brightly colored flowers give "**Dancing Flowers and Pinwheels**" a joyful, whimsical touch. Pinwheels lend even more energy. "Pick" flowers in colors that will enhance your favorite room.*

Dancing Flowers and Pinwheels

Quilt Size: 48" x 58" • Block Size: 10" square

Materials

- 20 bright prints, each at least 9" square
- 20 medium prints to coordinate with the brights, each at least 5" square
- 20 dark prints to coordinate with the bright and medium prints, each at least 2 1/2" square
- 1 yard light print for the background
- 1/2 yard light blue
- 1/2 yard dark green
- 1 1/2 yards medium blue for the border
- 3 yards backing fabric
- 52" x 62" piece of batting

Cutting

Dimensions include a 1/4" seam allowance.

From each bright print:
- Cut 4: 4 1/2" squares

From each medium print:
- Cut 4: 2 1/2" squares

From each dark print:
- Cut 1: 2 1/2" square

Also:
- Cut 10: 5 3/4" squares, light print
- Cut 80: 2 1/2" squares, light print
- Cut 10: 5 3/4" squares, light blue
- Cut 80: 2 1/2" squares, dark green
- Cut 4: 4 1/2" x 52" lengthwise strips, medium blue
- Cut 5: 2 1/2" x 50" lengthwise strips, medium blue, for the binding

Directions

1. Draw diagonal lines from corner to corner on the wrong side of each 5 3/4" light print square. Draw horizontal and vertical lines through the centers.

2. Place a marked 5 3/4" light print square on a 5 3/4" light blue square, right sides together. Sew 1/4" away from the diagonal lines on both sides. Make 10.

3. Cut the squares on the drawn lines to yield 80 pieced squares. Press the seam allowances toward the light blue. Set them aside.

4. Draw a diagonal line from corner to corner on the wrong side of each 2 1/2" light print and 2 1/2" medium print square.

For each block:

1. Place a marked 2 1/2" light print square on one corner of a 4 1/2" bright print square, and a marked 2 1/2" medium print square on the opposite corner. Sew on the drawn lines.

2. Press the squares toward the corners, aligning the edges. Trim the seam allowances to 1/4" to complete a square unit. Make 4.

3. Lay out a square unit, a 2 1/2" dark green square, and a pieced square. Sew them together to make a flower unit, as shown. Make 4.

Dancing Flowers and Pinwheels

4. Place a 2 1/2" dark print square on a flower unit, right sides together, as shown. Sew them together, stopping 1/2" from the bottom edge of the square. Press the seam allowance toward the flower unit.

5. Sew a flower unit to the top, as shown.

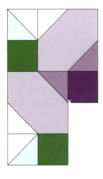

6. Sew a flower unit to the right side.

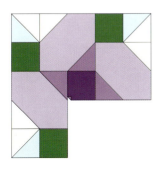

7. Sew a flower unit to the bottom, keeping the first unit free.

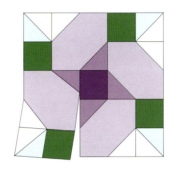

8. Finish sewing the first seam to complete the block. Make 20.

Assembly

1. Lay out the blocks in 5 rows of 4.

2. Sew the blocks into rows and join the rows.

3. Measure the length of the quilt. Trim 2 of the 4 1/2" x 52" medium blue strips to that measurement. Sew them to the long sides of the quilt.

4. Measure the width of the quilt, including the borders. Trim the remaining 4 1/2" x 52" medium blue strips to that measurement. Sew them to the remaining sides of the quilt.

5. Finish the quilt as described in the *General Directions*, using the 2 1/2" x 50" medium blue strips for the binding.

ALTERNATE COLOR IDEA

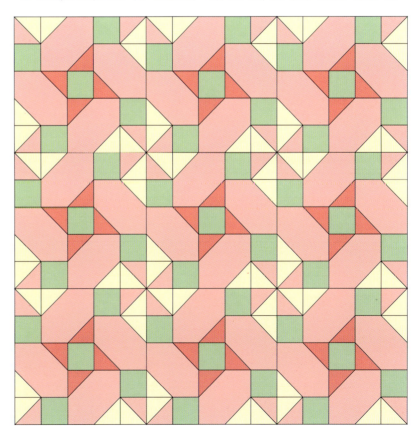

Star Magnolia

Bold blossoms present a visual treat in "**Star Magnolia.**" The circular 4-block design looks as if it might be difficult to make, but each small unit is alike and pieced with straight seams. It may be a bit time consuming but the finished look is spectacular. Make this quilt for a lovely "touch of spring" you'll enjoy year round.

STAR MAGNOLIA

Quilt Size: 56" square • Block Size: 24" square

Materials

- 1/3 yard light pink
- 1/2 yard medium rose
- 1/2 yard dark rose
- 1 1/4 yards white
- 2 yards dark blue/green
- 1 yard medium green
- 5/8 yard yellow
- 1/4 yard light blue
- 3 1/2 yards backing fabric
- 60" square of batting

Cutting

Patterns (page 17) are full size and include a 1/4" seam allowance as do all dimensions given. Cut the lengthwise dark blue strips before cutting other pieces from the same yardage.

From the light pink:
- Cut 16: B

From the medium rose:
- Cut 16: A
- Cut 16: AR
- Cut 16: 2 7/8" squares

From the dark rose:
- Cut 16: C
- Cut 16: CR

From the white:
- Cut 32: A
- Cut 32: AR
- Cut 64: 2 7/8" squares then cut 16 of them in half to yield 32 triangles
- Cut 64: 2 1/2" squares

From the dark blue:
- Cut 4: 2 1/2" x 60" lengthwise strips, for the binding
- Cut 2: 4 1/2" x 58" lengthwise strips
- Cut 2: 4 1/2" x 50" lengthwise strips
- Cut 16: A
- Cut 16: AR
- Cut 16: 2 7/8" squares

From the medium green:
- Cut 32: 2 1/2" x 6 1/2" rectangles
- Cut 32: 2 1/2" x 4 1/2" rectangles
- Cut 16: 2 1/2" squares

From the yellow:
- Cut 32: 2 1/2" x 4 1/2" rectangles
- Cut 16: 2 7/8" squares
- Cut 16: 2 1/2" squares

From the light blue:
- Cut 16: 2 7/8" squares

Directions

1. Draw a diagonal line from corner to corner on the wrong side of each 2 7/8" white square and each 2 7/8" yellow square.

2. Place a marked white square on a 2 7/8" medium rose square, right sides together. Sew 1/4" away from the drawn line on both sides. Make 16.

3. Cut the squares on the drawn lines to yield 32 pieced squares.

4. In the same manner, make 32 pieced squares using marked white squares and the 2 7/8" dark blue squares.

5. Make 32 pieced squares using the marked yellow squares and the 2 7/8" light blue squares.

6. Lay out 2 yellow/light blue pieced squares, a white/dark blue pieced square, and a 2 1/2" yellow square. Join them to make a Center unit. Make 16. Set them aside.

7. Sew a medium rose A and medium rose AR to a light pink B. Make 16.

Star Magnolia

8. Lay out one pieced unit, 2 white/medium rose pieced squares, a white/dark blue pieced square, and two 2 1/2" white squares. Sew them into sections and join the sections. Make 16.

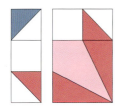

9. Sew a white triangle and a white A to a dark rose C. Sew a white triangle and a white AR to a dark rose CR. Make 16 of each.

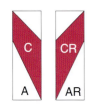

10. Sew one of each of these pieced units and a 2 1/2" medium green square to a pink/rose unit to make a Bud unit. Make 16. Set them aside.

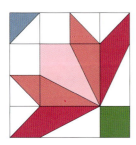

11. Sew a white A to a dark blue A. Sew a white AR to a dark blue AR. Make 16 of each.

12. Draw a diagonal line from corner to corner on the wrong side of each remaining 2 1/2" white square.

13. Place a marked square on a 2 1/2" x 6 1/2" medium green rectangle. Sew on the drawn line. Make 16 and 16 reversed, as shown.

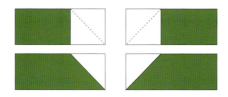

14. Place a 2 1/2" x 4 1/2" yellow rectangle on a 2 1/2" x 4 1/2" medium green rectangle, aligning the upper right corners, as shown. Sew from corner to corner. Open the unit and press the seam toward the green. Trim the seam allowance to 1/4". Make 16.

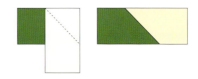

15. Make 16 reverse units using the remaining 2 1/2" x 4 1/2" yellow and medium green rectangles.

16. Lay out a white/green rectangle, a green/yellow rectangle, and a white/dark blue A unit. Join them to make a Side unit. Make 16.

17. Lay out the reverse units and join them to make a reverse Side unit. Make 16.

18. Lay out a Bud unit, Side unit, reverse Side unit, and a Center unit. Join them to make a quarter block. Make 16.

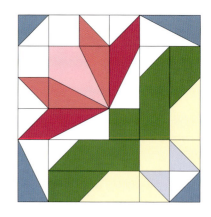

19. Join 4 quarter blocks to make a block. Make 4.

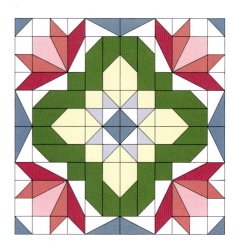

20. Sew the blocks into 2 rows of 2. Join the rows.

21. Measure the width of the quilt. Trim the 4 1/2" x 50" dark blue strips to that measurement. Sew them to opposite sides of the quilt.

22. Measure the length of the quilt, including the borders. Trim the 4 1/2" x 58" dark blue strips to that measurement. Sew them to the remaining sides of the quilt.

23. Finish the quilt as described in the *General Directions*, using the 2 1/2" x 60" dark blue strips for the binding.

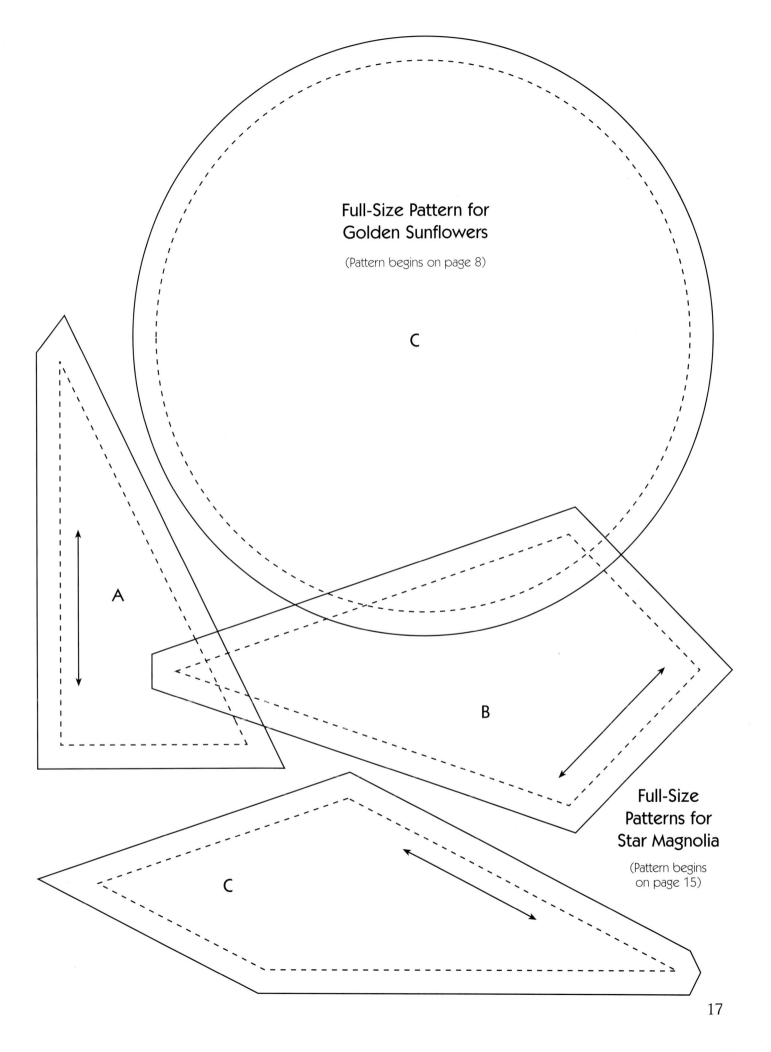

Friendship Star Flowers

A cycle of dynamic movement is sparked as Friendship Star patterns are set between Pinwheels in "**Friendship Star Flowers**."

Friendship Star Flower

Quilt Size: 72" square • Block Size: 12" square

Materials

- 2 yards dark green
- 2 1/2 yards medium green
- 1/2 yard light floral print
- 3/4 yard dark rose
- 3/4 yard light rose
- 2 yards beige
- 1/2 yard white
- 3/4 yard cranberry
- 4 1/2 yards backing fabric
- 76" square of batting

Cutting

Dimensions include a 1/4" seam allowance.

From the dark green:
- Cut 4: 1 1/2" x 64" lengthwise strips
- Cut 50: 4 7/8" squares

From the medium green:
Cut the lengthwise strips before cutting the squares.
- Cut 4: 2 1/2" x 76" lengthwise strips, for the binding
- Cut 2: 5 1/2" x 74" lengthwise strips
- Cut 2: 5 1/2" x 64" lengthwise strips
- Cut 50: 3 1/4" squares, then cut them in half diagonally to yield 100 triangles

From the light floral:
- Cut 25: 3 3/8" squares

From the dark rose:
- Cut 100: 2 1/2" squares

From the light rose:
- Cut 100: 2 1/2" squares

From the beige:
- Cut 50: 4 7/8" squares
- Cut 4: 1 1/2" x 40" strips
- Cut 100: 1 1/2" x 2 1/2" rectangles

From the white:
- Cut 8: 1 1/2" x 40" strips

From the cranberry:
- Cut 12: 1 1/2" x 40" strips

Directions

1. Center and sew 2 medium green triangles to opposite sides of a 3 3/8" light floral square, as shown. Press the seam allowances toward the triangles. Sew medium green triangles to the remaining sides. Press in the same manner to complete a center square. Make 25.

2. Trim each center square to 4 1/2". Set them aside.

3. Draw a diagonal line from corner to corner on the wrong side of each 4 7/8" beige square.

4. Place a marked square on a 4 7/8" dark green square, right sides together. Sew 1/4" away from the drawn line on both sides. Make 50.

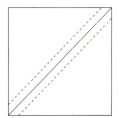

5. Cut the squares on the drawn lines to yield 100 large pieced squares. Press the seam allowances toward the green. Set them aside.

6. Sew a 1 1/2" x 40" white strip to a 1 1/2" x 40" cranberry strip along their length. Make 8. Press the seam allowances toward the cranberry.

FRIENDSHIP STAR FLOWER

7. Cut twenty-five 1 1/2" sections from each pieced strip.

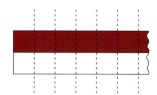

8. Sew 2 sections together to make a Four Patch. Make 100.

9. Sew a 1 1/2" x 40" beige strip to a 1 1/2" x 40" cranberry strip. Make 4. Press, as before.

10. Cut twenty-five 1 1/2" sections from each pieced strip.

11. Sew a section to a 1 1/2" x 2 1/2" beige rectangle to make a small pieced square, as shown. Make 100.

12. Lay out a small pieced square, a Four Patch, and two 2 1/2" dark rose squares. Sew them into pairs and join the pairs to make a large Four Patch. Make 50.

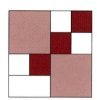

13. In the same manner, make 50 large Four Patches using the 2 1/2" light rose squares.

14. Lay out a center square, 4 large pieced squares, 2 large dark rose Four Patches, and 2 large light rose Four Patches. Sew them into rows and join the rows to make a block. Make 25.

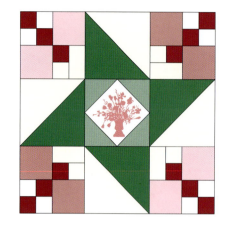

Assembly

1. Referring to the photo, lay out the blocks in 5 rows of 5, turning them to form light and dark rose colored flowers.

2. Measure the length of the quilt. Trim 2 of the 1 1/2" x 64" dark green strips to that measurement. Sew them to opposite sides of the quilt.

3. Measure the width of the quilt, including the borders. Trim the remaining 1 1/2" x 64" dark green strips to that measurement. Sew them to the remaining sides of the quilt.

4. In the same manner, trim the 5 1/2" x 64" medium green strips to fit the quilt's length. Sew them to opposite sides of the quilt.

5. Trim the 5 1/2" x 74" medium green strips to fit the quilt's width and sew them to the remaining sides of the quilt.

6. Finish the quilt as described in the *General Directions*, using the 2 1/2" x 76" medium green strips for the binding.

ALTERNATE COLOR IDEA

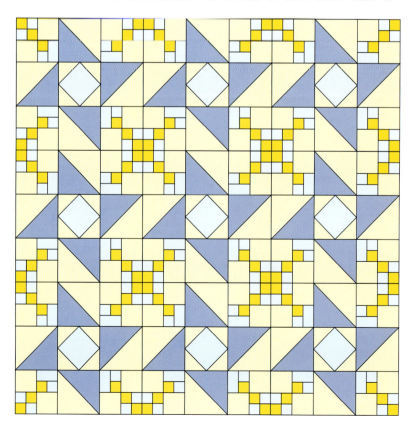

Pinwheel Garden

It's hard to believe that a single repeated block design produces the explosion of patterns and color of "Pinwheel Garden."

Pinwheel Garden

Quilt Size: 56" square • Block Size: 16" square

Materials

- 2 yards dark blue
- 1/2 yard medium blue
- 1 yard light blue
- 1/2 yard dark green
- 1 yard medium green
- 3/4 yard white
- 1 1/4 yards beige
- 5/8 yard dark pink
- 3 1/2 yards backing fabric
- 60" square of batting

Cutting

Pattern A (page 10) is full size and includes a 1/4" seam allowance as do all dimensions given.

From the dark blue:
- Cut 4: 4 1/2" x 58" lengthwise strips
- Cut 5: 2 1/2" x 50" lengthwise strips, for the binding
- Cut 9: 3 1/4" squares, then cut them in quarters diagonally to yield 36 triangles
- Cut 36: 2 1/2" squares

From the medium blue:
- Cut 36: 2 1/2" x 4 1/2" rectangles

From the light blue:
- Cut 36: 2 1/2" x 4 1/2" rectangles
- Cut 9: 3 1/4" squares, then cut them in quarters diagonally to yield 36 triangles

From the dark green:
- Cut 72: 2 1/2" squares

From the medium green:
- Cut 36: 2 1/2" x 4 1/2" rectangles
- Cut 36: 2 1/2" x 6 1/2" rectangles

From the white:
- Cut 72: 2 1/2" squares
- Cut 36: 2 7/8" squares, then cut them in half diagonally to yield 72 triangles

From the beige:
- Cut 36: 2 1/2" x 4 1/2" rectangles
- Cut 36: 2 1/2" x 6 1/2" rectangles
- Cut 18: 3 1/4" squares, then cut them in half diagonally to yield 72 triangles

From the dark pink:
- Cut 36: A
- Cut 36: AR

Directions

1. Sew a dark blue triangle to a beige triangle to make a pieced triangle. Sew a light blue triangle to a beige triangle in the same manner. Make 36 of each, as shown.

2. Sew a white triangle to a dark pink AR. Sew a dark blue pieced triangle to the unit, as shown. Make 36.

3. Sew a white triangle to a dark pink A. Sew a light blue pieced triangle to the unit, as shown. Make 36.

4. Sew 2 units together to make a Bud unit. Make 36. Set them aside.

5. Draw a diagonal line from corner to corner on the wrong side of each 2 1/2" white square and each 2 1/2" dark green square.

6. Place a marked white square on

Pinwheel Garden

a 2 1/2" x 4 1/2" medium green rectangle. Sew on the drawn line, as shown. Press the square toward the corner, aligning the edges. Trim the seam allowance to 1/4". Make 36.

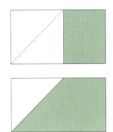

7. Make 36 pieced rectangles in the same manner, using 2 1/2" dark green squares and 2 1/2" x 4 1/2" beige rectangles. Set them aside.

8. Place a 2 1/2" x 6 1/2" medium green rectangle on a 2 1/2" x 4 1/2" light blue rectangle, aligning the edges, as shown. Sew from corner to corner. Trim 1/4" beyond the stitching. Press the seam allowance toward the green.

9. Place a marked 2 1/2" white square on the opposite end of the green rectangle. Sew on the drawn line. Press the square toward the corner, aligning the edges. Trim the seam allowance to 1/4".

10. Sew a green/white pieced rectangle and a green/beige pieced rectangle to a Bud unit. Sew a green/white/blue pieced rectangle to the bottom. Make 36. Set them aside.

11. Place a marked 2 1/2" dark green square on a 2 1/2" x 6 1/2" beige rectangle. Sew on the marked line. Press the square toward the corner and trim the seam allowance to 1/4".

12. Place a 2 1/2" x 4 1/2" medium blue rectangle on the opposite end of the beige rectangle. Sew from corner to corner. Trim 1/4" beyond the stitching and press the seam allowance toward the blue.

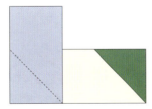

13. Place a marked 2 1/2" dark blue square on the other end of the medium blue rectangle. Sew on the marked line. Press the square toward the corner and trim the seam allowance to 1/4". Make 36.

14. Sew a pieced strip to each bud unit.

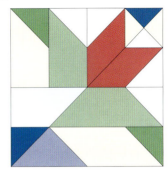

15. Sew 4 bud units together to make a block. Make 9.

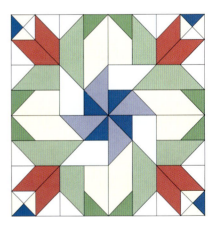

Assembly

1. Lay out the blocks in 3 rows of 3.

2. Sew the blocks into rows and join the rows.

3. Center and sew the 4 1/2" x 58" dark blue strips to the sides of the quilt. Start, stop, and backstitch at the 1/4" seamlines.

4. Miter the corners as described in the *General Directions*.

5. Finish the quilt as described in the *General Directions*, using the 2 1/2" x 50" dark blue strips for the binding.

Iris Garden

Enchanting irises, in shades of lavender, orchid, light blue, and yellow, are one of the most favored garden flowers around the world. Make your own "Iris Garden" using any colors you would find in irises.

Iris Garden

Quilt Size: 60" x 84" • Block Size: 16" x 24"

Materials

- Assorted light, medium, and dark prints in lavender, orchid, light blue, and yellow for the irises
- 2 1/2 yards pale yellow for the background
- Assorted greens for the leaves
- 1 1/2 yards light blue
- 2 3/4 yards dark violet
- 1/4 yard bright yellow
- 1/4 yard bright gold
- 2 1/2 yards dark fabric for the border
- 5 yards backing fabric
- 64" x 88" piece of batting

Cutting

Appliqué patterns F and G are full size and do not include a seam allowance. Make a template for each piece. Trace around the templates on the right side of the fabric and add a 1/8" to 3/16" seam allowance to the pieces as you cut them out. All other dimensions include a 1/4" seam allowance.

For each of 9 blocks:
- Cut 1 each A and AR, light iris fabric
- Cut 1: 6 7/8" square, light iris fabric, then cut it in half diagonally to yield 2 triangles
- Cut 1: C, medium iris fabric
- Cut 1: B, dark iris fabric

From the pale yellow:
- Cut 9: 8 7/8" squares, then cut them in half diagonally to yield 18 large triangles
- Cut 3: 5 1/4" squares, then cut them in quarters diagonally to yield 12 small triangles. You will use 9.
- Cut 23: 4 7/8" squares, then cut them in half diagonally to yield 46 medium triangles
- Cut 18: 2 1/2" squares
- Cut 9: D
- Cut 9: 2 1/2" x 16 1/2" strips
- Cut 18: 2 1/2" x 14 1/2" strips

From the assorted greens:
- Cut 5: 5 1/4" squares, then cut them in quarters diagonally to yield 20 large triangles. You will use 18.
- Cut 9: 2 7/8" squares, then cut them in half diagonally to yield 18 small triangles
- Cut 9: 3/4" x 4 1/2" strips
- Cut 9 each: E and ER

From the light blue:
- Cut 6: 2 1/2" x 24 1/2" strips
- Cut 2: 2 1/2" x 52 1/2" strips

From the dark border fabric:
- Cut 2: 4 1/2" x 86" strips
- Cut 2: 4 1/2" x 62" strips
- Cut 4: 2 1/2" x 80" strips, for the binding

From the bright gold:
- Cut 9: F

From the bright yellow:
- Cut 9: G

Directions

For each block:

1. Sew a small pale yellow triangle to a dark B. Sew a medium pale yellow triangle to the unit.

2. Sew a light A and light AR to the first unit, pivoting at the dots.

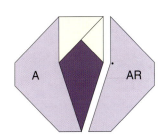

3. Sew a medium pale yellow triangle to each corner of the unit to complete Unit 1.

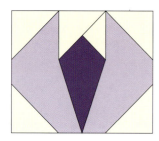

4. Appliqué a gold F and a bright yellow G to a medium C. Sew large green triangles to the unit to make a pieced triangle.

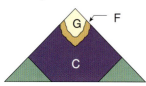

5. Draw a diagonal line from corner to corner on the wrong side of two 2 1/2" pale yellow squares. Place a square on the right angle corner of a light triangle, right sides together. Sew on the drawn line.

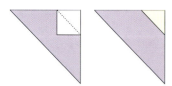

6. Press the square toward the corner, aligning the edges. Trim the seam allowance to 1/4". Make 2. Sew the units to the pieced triangle to complete Unit 2.

7. Press the long edges of a 3/4" x 4 1/2" green strip 1/4" toward the wrong side. Trim 1/8" from each long edge. Appliqué the strip to a pale yellow D.

8. Sew a green print E and ER to the long sides of the D, stopping and backstitching at the dot. Sew the bottom seam, joining the E and ER to complete Unit 3.

9. Join Units 1, 2, and 3. Sew a small green triangle to each of two 2 1/2" x 14 1/2" pale yellow strips and sew the strips to the sides of the iris unit.

10. Sew a 2 1/2" x 16 1/2" pale yellow strip to the top of the iris. Sew a large pale yellow triangle to each bottom corner to complete the block. Make 9.

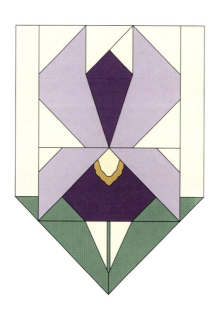

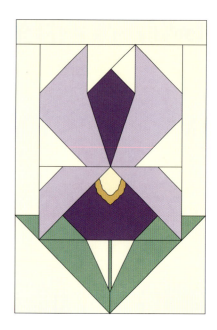

Assembly

1. Lay out the blocks in 3 rows of 3. Place the 2 1/2" x 24 1/2" strips between the blocks in the rows. Sew the blocks and strips into rows.
2. Sew the rows and 2 1/2" x 52 1/2" light blue strips together alternately.
3. Sew the 4 1/2" x 86" dark strips to the long sides of the quilt. Start, stop and backstitch 1/4" from the edges of the quilt.
4. Sew the 4 1/2" x 62" dark strips to the remaining sides of the quilt in the same manner.
5. Miter the corners as described in the *General Directions*.
6. Finish the quilt as described in the *General Directions*, using the 2 1/2" x 80" dark strips for the binding.

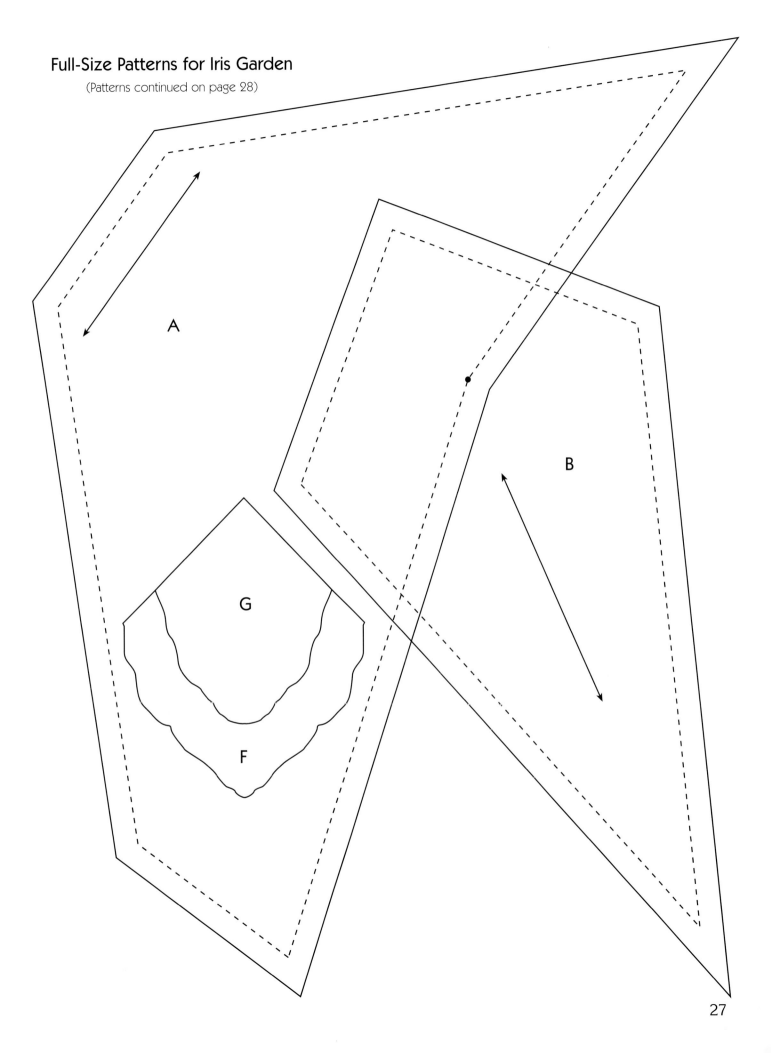

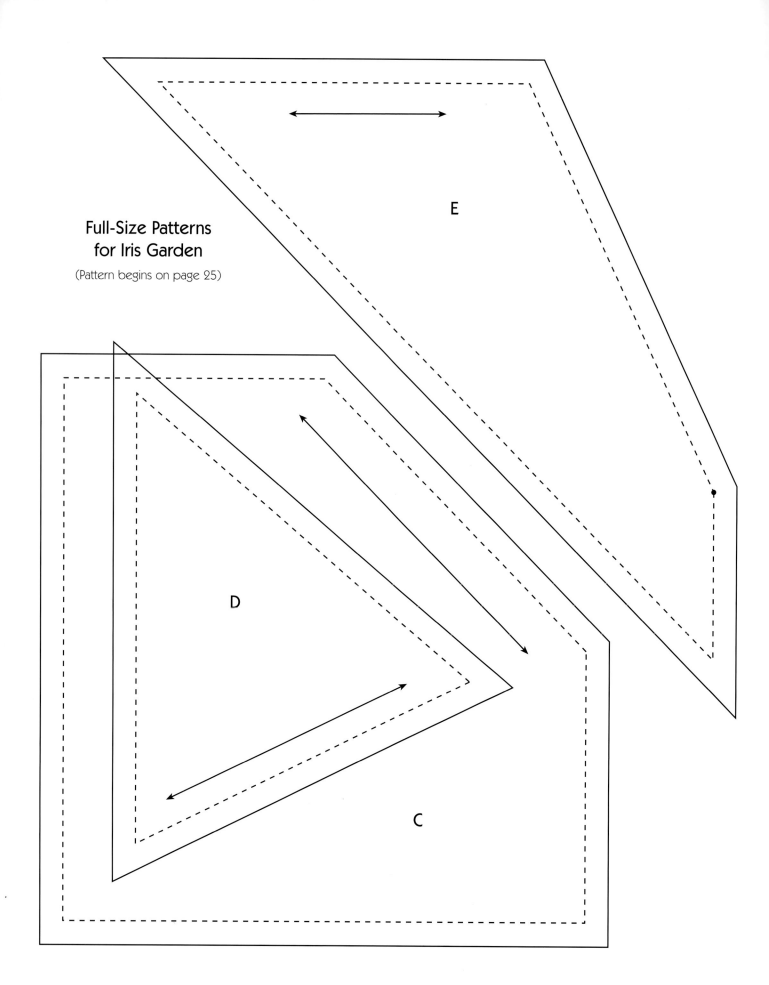

Circle of Tulips

This colorful design makes a happy spring quilt. Use up some of the leftover pieces in your scrap bag or purchase some new gotta-have fabric! Either way, you'll love the result.

Circle of Tulips

Quilt Size: 44" square • Block Size: 12" square

Materials

- Assorted bright prints for the buds each at least 2" x 5" and totaling at least 3/4 yard
- 9 assorted green prints for the leaves each at least 6" x 12"
- 1 1/2 yards dark green
- 1 1/2 yards dark red
- 2 yards white
- 1/4 yard light gold
- 2 3/4 yards backing fabric
- 48" square of batting

Cutting

Patterns are full size and include a 1/4" seam allowance as do all dimensions given.
- Cut 4: 3 1/2" x 46" strips, dark green
- Cut 5: 2 1/2" x 40" strips, dark green for the binding
- Cut 4: 1 1/2" x 46" strips, dark red
- Cut 36: A, white
- Cut 36: AR, white
- Cut 36: 2 7/8" squares, white, then cut them in half diagonally to yield 72 triangles
- Cut 36: C, white
- Cut 18: 2 7/8" squares, light gold
- Cut 36: B, assorted bright prints
- Cut 36: BR, assorted bright prints
- Cut 36: D, assorted bright prints

From each green print:
- Cut 4 each: A (page 10) and AR
- Cut 2: 2 7/8" squares

Directions

1. Sew a bright print D to a white C to make a corner unit, as shown. Make 36.

2. Sew a bright print B to a bright print BR, as shown, stopping at the dot, and backstitching. Make 36.

3. Set a corner unit from the same color family into a B/BR unit, as shown. Sew 2 white triangles to the unit to make a Bud unit. Make 36.

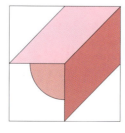

4. Sew a white A to a green print A. Sew a white AR to a green print AR. Make 36 of each.

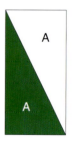 

5. Draw a diagonal line from corner to corner on the wrong side of each 2 7/8" light gold square.

6. Place a marked square on a 2 7/8" green print square, right sides together. Sew 1/4" away from the diagonal line on both sides. Make 18.

7. Cut the squares on the drawn lines to yield 36 pieced squares.

8. Lay out 4 Bud units, 4 pieced squares, 4 A units and 4 AR units, matching the green prints on opposite sides of the block, as shown.

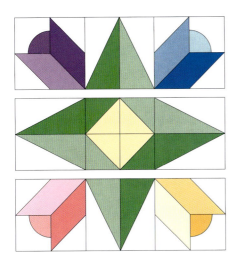

9. Sew A and AR units into pairs. Sew the pieced squares into a Four Patch for the center.

10. Sew the sections together to complete a block. Make 9.

Assembly

1. Lay out the blocks in 3 rows of 3. Sew the blocks into rows and join the rows.

2. Sew a 1 1/2" x 46" dark red strip to a 3 1/2" x 46" dark green strip along their length. Make 4.

3. Sew the borders to the sides of the quilt. Start, stop, and backstitch at the 1/4" seamlines.

4. Miter the corners according to the *General Directions*.

5. Finish the quilt as described in the *General Directions*, using the 2 1/2" x 40" dark green strips for the binding.

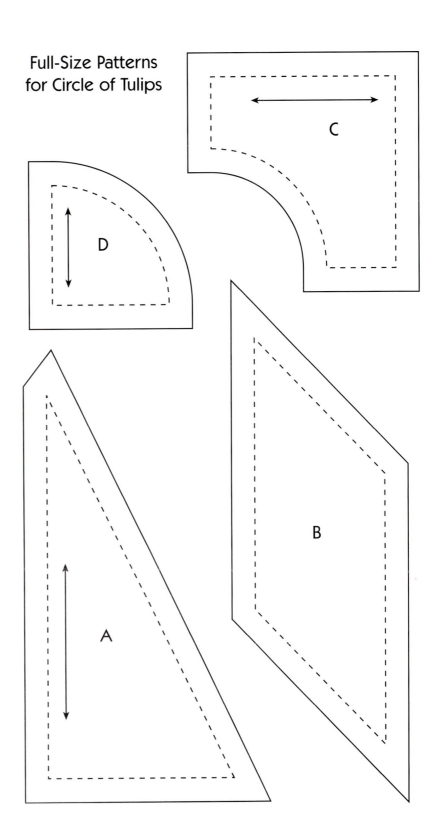

Full-Size Patterns for Circle of Tulips

General Directions

ABOUT THE PATTERNS

Read through the pattern directions before cutting fabric. Yardage requirements are based on fabric with a useable width of 40". Pattern directions are given in step-by-step order. If you are sending your quilt to a professional machine quilter, consult them regarding the necessary batting and backing size for your quilt. Batting and backing dimensions listed in the patterns are for hand quilting.

FABRICS

We suggest using 100% cotton. Wash fabric in warm water with mild detergent and no fabric softener. Dry fabric on a warm-to-hot setting. Press with a hot dry iron to remove any wrinkles.

TEMPLATES

Template patterns are full size and, unless otherwise noted, include a 1/4" seam allowance. The solid line is the cutting line; the dashed line is the stitching line. Place a sheet of firm, clear template plastic over the patterns and trace the cutting line and/or stitching line for each one. Also trace the grainline if there is one. Templates for machine piecing include a seam allowance, templates for hand piecing generally do not.

MARKING THE FABRIC

Test marking tools for removability before using them. Sharpen pencils often. Align the grainline on the template with the grainline of the fabric. Place a piece of fine sandpaper beneath the fabric to prevent slipping, if desired. For machine piecing, mark the right side of the fabric. For hand piecing, mark the wrong side of the fabric, and flip asymmetrical templates before tracing them. Mark and cut just enough pieces to make a sample block and piece it to be sure your templates are accurate.

PIECING

For machine piecing, sew 12 stitches per inch, exactly 1/4" from the edge of the fabric. To make accurate piecing easier, mark the throat plate with a piece of tape 1/4" away from the point where the needle pierces the fabric. Start and stop stitching at the cut edges except for set-in pieces. For set-ins, start and stop at the 1/4" seamlines and backstitch.

For hand piecing, begin with a small knot. Make one small backstitch and continue with a small running stitch, backstitching every 3-4 stitches. Stitch directly on the marked line from point to point, not edge to edge. Finish with 2 or 3 small backstitches before cutting the thread.

MITERED BORDERS

Measure the length of the quilt top and add 2 times the border width plus 2". Cut border strips that measurement. Match the center of the quilt top with the center of the border strip and pin to the corners. Stitch, beginning and ending each seamline 1/4" from the edge of the quilt top. After all borders have been attached, miter one corner at a time. With the quilt top right side down, lay one border over the other. Draw a straight line at a 45° angle from the inner to the outer corner.

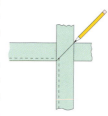

Reverse the positions of the borders and mark another corner-to-corner line. With the borders right sides together and the marked seamlines carefully matched, stitch from the inner to the outer corner. Open the mitered seam to make sure it lies flat, then trim excess fabric and press.

PRESSING

Press with a dry iron. Press seam allowances toward the darker of the two pieces whenever possible. Otherwise, trim away 1/16" from the darker seam allowance to prevent it from showing through. Press all blocks, sashings, and borders before assembling the quilt top.

FINISHING YOUR QUILT

Mark your quilt design before basting the quilt top together with the batting and backing. Chalk pencils show well on dark fabrics, otherwise use a very hard (#3 or #4) pencil or other marker for this purpose. Test your marker first.

Transfer paper designs by placing fabric over the design and tracing. A light box may be necessary for darker fabrics. Precut plastic stencils that fit the area you wish to quilt may be placed on top of the quilt and traced. Use a ruler to mark straight, even grids. Masking tape can also be used to mark straight lines. Temporary quilting stencils can be made from clear adhesive-backed paper or freezer paper and reused many times. To avoid residue, do not leave tape or adhesive-backed paper on your quilt overnight.

Outline quilting does not require marking. Simply eyeball 1/4" from the seam or stitch "in the ditch" next to the seam. To prevent uneven stitching, try to avoid quilting through seam allowances wherever possible.

BINDING

Cut binding strips with the grain for straight-edge quilts. To make 1/2" finished binding, cut 2 1/2"-wide strips. Sew the strips together with diagonal seams; trim and press the seam allowances open.

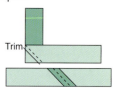

Fold the strip in half lengthwise, wrong side in, and press. Position the strip on the right side of the quilt top, aligning the raw edges of the binding with the edge of the quilt top. Leaving 6" of the binding strip free and beginning a few inches from one corner, stitch the binding to the quilt with a 1/4" seam allowance. When you reach a corner, stop stitching 1/4" from the edge of the quilt top and backstitch. Clip the threads and remove the quilt from the machine. Fold the binding up and away from the quilt, forming a 45° angle, as shown. Keeping the angled fold secure, fold the binding back down. This fold should be even with the edge of the quilt top. Begin stitching at the fold.

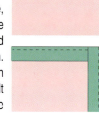

Continue stitching around the quilt in this manner to within 6" of the starting point. To finish, fold both strips back along the edge of the quilt so that the folded edges meet about 3" from both lines of stitching and the binding lies flat on the quilt. Finger press to crease the folds. Measure the width of the folded binding. Cut the strips that distance beyond the folds. (In this case 1 1/4" beyond the folds.)

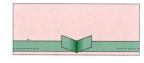

Open both strips and place the ends at right angles to each other, right sides together. Fold the bulk of the quilt out of your way. Join the strips with a diagonal seam as shown.

Trim the seam allowance to 1/4" and press it open. Refold the strip wrong side in. Place the binding flat against the quilt, and finish stitching it to the quilt. Trim excess batting and backing so that the binding edge will be filled with batting when you fold the binding to the back of the quilt. Blindstitch the binding to the back, covering the seamline.

Remove visible markings. Sign and date your quilt.